A · SELECTION · OF
ANIMAL · POEMS

BIRDS
BEASTS
A·N·D
FISHES

ILLUSTRATED BY
REG CARTWRIGHT
POEMS SELECTED BY
ANNE CARTER

WALKER BOOKS

LONDON

INTRODUCTION

Animals have always been a part of man's world and mankind has looked on them variously as threat, as nuisance, as food, as useful servants, objects of pride or entertainment and even, now and then, as friends. For the most part, down the ages, we have had little difficulty in getting the better of them and have seen no reason why their needs should not be subordinate to our convenience. We have made them victims of our thoughtless cruelty and abused their habitats at will. We have no right to be proud of ourselves.

Now, as we begin to glimpse, at last, the destruction that we are wreaking on our planet, the humbling thought may yet occur to us that one osprey or one elephant could have more to offer the earth than any number of our arrogant selves. It will not alter our behaviour. Survival is, after all, a prime law of the jungle. But it may just make us look a little closer.

Taking a closer look has been the business of poets down the ages. They watch, they listen and record, with joy and wonder, pity and respect and, very often, laughter. Even when using animals only to point a moral or express some human feeling, poetry can focus on a tiny detail, a look or movement, and lay it, living, before our eyes. The Roman poet Boethius, himself in prison, identified with a captive bird and his words, beautifully translated by Helen Waddell, speak just as directly to us today. John Clare's vixen, two centuries dead, might play in a suburban garden now. William Blake's tiger and Ted Hughes' jaguar meet in our terror and delight.

The birds, beasts and fishes in this collection were chosen for their own sake, because of a special quality in each poem. It was a difficult choice because there were so many more we might have included. We could have made a book of cats alone. But our aim was to portray a living world whose vigour and variety would be visually complemented by the illustrations. This world belongs to all of us. The poems are our key to looking closer.

Anne Carter

Reg Cartwright

THE EAGLE

He clasps the crag with crooked hands
Close to the sun in lonely lands,
Ringed with the azure world, he stands.

The wrinkled sea beneath him crawls;
He watches from his mountain walls,
And like a thunderbolt he falls.

ALFRED, LORD TENNYSON

A VISIT FROM THE SEA

Far from the loud sea beaches
    Where he goes fishing and crying,
Here in the inland garden
    Why is the sea-gull flying?

Here are no fish to dive for;
    Here is the corn and lea;
Here are the green trees rustling.
    Hie away home to sea!

Fresh is the river water
    And quiet among the rushes;
This is no home for the sea-gull
    But for the rooks and thrushes.

Pity the bird that has wandered!
    Pity the sailor ashore!
Hurry him home to the ocean,
    Let him come here no more!

High on the sea-cliff ledges
    The white gulls are trooping and crying,
Here among rooks and roses,
    Why is the sea-gull flying?

ROBERT LOUIS STEVENSON

7

THE VULTURE

The Vulture eats between his meals
   And that's the reason why
He very, very rarely feels
   As well as you and I.

His eye is dull, his head is bald,
   His neck is growing thinner.
Oh! what a lesson for us all
   To only eat at dinner!

HILAIRE BELLOC

The robin and the wren,
They fought upon the porridge pan,
But ere the robin got the spoon,
The wren had eat the porridge down.

ANON.

PIGEON AND WREN

Coo-oo! Coo-oo!
It's as much as a pigeon can do
    To maintain two.
But the little wren can maintain ten,
And bring them all up like gentlemen.

ANON.

THE CORMORANT

The common cormorant or shag
Lays eggs inside a paper bag,
The reason you will see no doubt –
It is to keep the lightning out.
But what these unobservant birds
Have never noticed is that herds
Of wandering bears may come with buns
And steal the bags to hold the crumbs.

CHRISTOPHER ISHERWOOD

THE PELICAN CHORUS

King and Queen of the Pelicans we;
No other Birds so grand we see!
None but we have feet like fins!
With lovely leathery throats and chins!
  Ploffskin, Pluffskin, Pelican jee!
  We think no Birds so happy as we!
  Plumpskin, Ploshkin, Pelican jill!
  We think so then, and we thought so still!

We live on the Nile. The Nile we love.
By night we sleep on the cliffs above;
By day we fish, and at eve we stand
On long bare islands of yellow sand.
And when the sun sinks slowly down
And the great rock walls grow dark and brown,
Where the purple river rolls fast and dim
And the Ivory Ibis starlike skim,
Wing to wing we dance around, –
Stamping our feet with a flumpy sound, –
Opening our mouths as Pelicans ought,
And this is the song we nightly snort; –
  Ploffskin, Pluffskin, Pelican jee! –
  We think no Birds so happy as we!
  Plumpskin, Ploshkin, Pelican jill, –
  We think so then, and we thought so still.

Last year came out our Daughter, Dell;
And all the Birds received her well.
To do her honour, a feast we made
For every bird that can swim or wade.
Herons and Gulls, and Cormorants black,
Cranes, and Flamingoes with scarlet back,
Plovers and Storks, and Geese in clouds,
Swans and Dilberry Ducks in crowds.
Thousands of Birds in wondrous flight!
They ate and drank and danced all night,
And echoing back from the rocks you heard
Multitude-echoes from Bird and Bird, –
  Ploffskin, Pluffskin, Pelican jee,
  We think no Birds so happy as we!
  Plumpskin, Ploshkin, Pelican jill,
  We think so then, and we thought so still!

Yes, they came; and among the rest,
The King of the Cranes all grandly dressed.
Such a lovely tail! Its feathers float
Between the ends of his blue dress-coat;

With pea-green trowsers all neat,
And a delicate frill to hide his feet, –
(For though no one speaks of it, every one knows,
He has got no webs between his toes!)

As soon as he saw our Daughter Dell,
In violent love that Crane King fell, –
On seeing her waddling form so fair,
With a wreath of shrimps in her short white hair.
And before the end of the next long day,
Our Dell had given her heart away;
For the King of the Cranes had won that heart,
With a Crocodile's egg and a large fish-tart.
She vowed to marry the King of the Cranes,
Leaving the Nile for stranger plains;
And away they flew in a gathering crowd
Of endless birds in a lengthening cloud.
   Ploffskin, Pluffskin, Pelican jee,
   We think no Birds so happy as we!
   Plumpskin, Ploshkin, Pelican jill,
   We think so then, and we thought so still!

And far away in the twilight sky,
We heard them singing a lessening cry, –
Farther and farther till out of sight,
And we stood alone in the silent night!
Often since, in the nights of June,
We sit on the sand and watch the moon; –
She has gone to the great Gromboolian plain,
And we probably never shall meet again!
Oft, in the long still nights of June,
We sit on the rocks and watch the moon; –

– She dwells by the streams of the Chankly Bore,
And we probably never shall see her more.
   Ploffskin, Pluffskin, Pelican jee,
   We think no Birds so happy as we!
   Plumpskin, Ploshkin, Pelican jill,
   We think so then, and we thought so still!

EDWARD LEAR

THE TWA CORBIES

As I was walking all alane,
I heard twa corbies making a mane,
And tane unto the tither say:–
"Where sall we gang and dine to-day?"

"– In behint yon auld fail dyke,
I wat there lies a new-slain Knight;
And naebody kens that he lies there
But his hawk, his hound, and lady fair.

"His hound is to the hunting gane,
His hawk to fetch the wild-fowl hame,
His lady's ta'en another mate,
So we may mak our dinner sweet.

"Ye'll sit on his white hause-bane,
And I'll pick out his bonnie blue een.
Wi' ae lock o' his gowden hair
We'll theek our nest when it grows bare.

"Mony a one for him maks mane,
But nane sall ken where he is gane.
O'er his white banes, where they are bare,
The wind sall blaw for evermair."

ANON.

SWEET SUFFOLK OWL

Sweet Suffolk owl, so trimly dight,
With feathers like a lady bright,
Thou singest alone, sitting by night,
– Te whit, te whoo, te whit, to whit.
Thy note, that forth so freely rolls,
With shrill command the mouse controls,
And sings a dirge for dying souls,
– Te whit, te whoo, te whit, to whit.

ANON.

CAPTIVE BIRD

This bird was happy once in the high trees.
You cage it in your cellar, bring it seed,
Honey to sip, all that its heart can need
Or human love can think of: till it sees,
Leaping too high within its narrow room
The old familiar shadow of the leaves,
And spurns the seed with tiny desperate claws.
Naught but the woods despairing pleads,
The woods, the woods again, it grieves, it grieves.

BOETHIUS
Translated from the Latin by
HELEN WADDELL

THE WINDHOVER

To Christ our Lord

I caught this morning morning's minion, king-
   dom of daylight's dauphin, dapple-dawn-drawn
     Falcon, in his riding
   Of the rolling level underneath him steady air, and
     striding
High there, how he rung upon the rein of a wimpling
     wing
In his ecstasy! then off, off forth on swing,
   As a skate's heel sweeps smooth on a bow-bend: the
hurl and gliding
   Rebuffed the big wind. My heart in hiding
Stirred for a bird, – the achieve of, the mastery of the
     thing!

Brute beauty and valour and act, oh, air, pride, plume,
     here
   Buckle! AND the fire that breaks from thee then, a
     billion
Times told lovelier, more dangerous, O my chevalier!

   No wonder of it: shéer plód makes plough down
     sillion
Shine, and blue-bleak embers, ah my dear,
   Fall, gall themselves, and gash gold-vermilion.

GERARD MANLEY HOPKINS

Answer To A Child's Question

Do you ask what the birds say? The Sparrow, the Dove,
The Linnet and Thrush say, "I love and I love!"
In the winter they're silent – the wind is so strong;
What it says, I don't know, but it sings a loud song.
But green leaves, and blossoms, and sunny warm weather,
And singing, and loving – all come back together.
But the Lark is so brimful of gladness and love,
The green fields below him, the blue sky above,
That he sings, and he sings; and for ever sings he –
"I love my Love, and my Love loves me!"

SAMUEL TAYLOR COLERIDGE

16

An Epitaph On A Robin Redbreast

Tread lightly here, for here, 'tis said,
When piping winds are hush'd around,
A small note wakes from underground,
Where now his tiny bones are laid.

No more in lone and leafless groves,
With ruffled wing and faded breast,
His friendless, homeless spirit roves;
– Gone to the world where birds are blest!
Where never cat glides o'er the green,
Or school-boy's giant form is seen;
But Love, and Joy, and smiling Spring
Inspire their little souls to sing!

SAMUEL ROGERS

THE OWL

When cats run home and light is come,
   And dew is cold upon the ground,
And the far-off stream is dumb,
   And the whirring sail goes round,
   And the whirring sail goes round;
     Alone and warming his five wits,
     The white owl in the belfry sits.

When merry milkmaids click the latch,
   And rarely smells the new-mown hay,
And the cock hath sung beneath the thatch
   Twice or thrice his roundelay,
   Twice or thrice his roundelay;
     Alone and warming his five wits,
     The white owl in the belfry sits.

ALFRED, LORD TENNYSON

NIGHT HERON

Hunting my cat along the evening brook
Where she'd been stalking deer mice in the weeds,
I nearly missed this sight – the great night heron
Bluer than dusk in the maze of willow reeds.

Beautiful, motionless, he stood in silence
On one leg, waiting for lantern flies,
And gazed across the brook to where in hemlock
His nest of sticks rose high against the skies.

Then at my feet I saw my fierce young hunter
Crouched in the wet grass, trembling and in awe.
We left our heron to his stars. Cat shivered
And touched my cheek with a damp and golden paw.

FRANCES FROST

Kill a robin or a wren,
Never prosper, boy or man.

ANON.

Crow on the fence,
Rain will go hence.
Crow on the ground,
Rain will come down.

ANON.

In marble halls as white as milk,
Lined with a skin as soft as silk,
Within a fountain crystal-clear,
A golden apple doth appear.
No doors there are to this stronghold,
Yet thieves break in and steal the gold.

ANON.

THE MANOEUVRE

I saw the two starlings
coming in toward the wires.
But at the last,
just before alighting, they

turned in the air together
and landed backwards!
that's what got me – to
face into the wind's teeth.

WILLIAM CARLOS WILLIAMS

THE WASP

Where the ripe pears droop heavily
   The yellow wasp hums loud and long
   His hot and drowsy autumn song:
A yellow flame he seems to be,
   When darting suddenly from high
   He lights where fallen peaches lie:

Yellow and black, this tiny thing's
A tiger-soul on elfin wings.

WILLIAM SHARP

THE BAT

Lightless, unholy, eldritch thing,
Whose murky and erratic wing
Swoops so sickeningly, and whose
Aspect to the female Muse
Is a demon's, made of stuff
Like tattered, sooty waterproof,
Looking dirty, clammy, cold.

Wicked, poisonous, and old:
I have maligned thee! . . . for the Cat
Lately caught a little bat,
Seized it softly, bore it in.
On the carpet, dark as sin
In the lamplight, painfully
It limped about, and could not fly.

Even fear must yield to love,
And Pity makes the depths to move.
Though sick with horror, I must stoop,
Grasp it gently, take it up,
And carry it, and place it where
It could resume the twilight air.

Strange revelation! warm as milk,
Clean as a flower, smooth as silk!
O what a piteous face appears,
What great fine thin translucent ears!
What chestnut down and crapy wings,
Finer than any lady's things –
And O a little one that clings!

Warm, clean, and lovely, though not fair,
And burdened with a mother's care:
Go hunt the hurtful fly, and bear
My blessing to your kind in air.

RUTH PITTER

FLYING CROOKED

The butterfly, a cabbage-white,
(His honest idiocy of flight)
Will never now, it is too late,
Master the art of flying straight,
Yet has – who knows so well as I? –
A just sense of how not to fly:
He lurches here and here by guess
And God and hope and hopelessness.
Even the aerobatic swift
Has not his flying-crooked gift.

ROBERT GRAVES

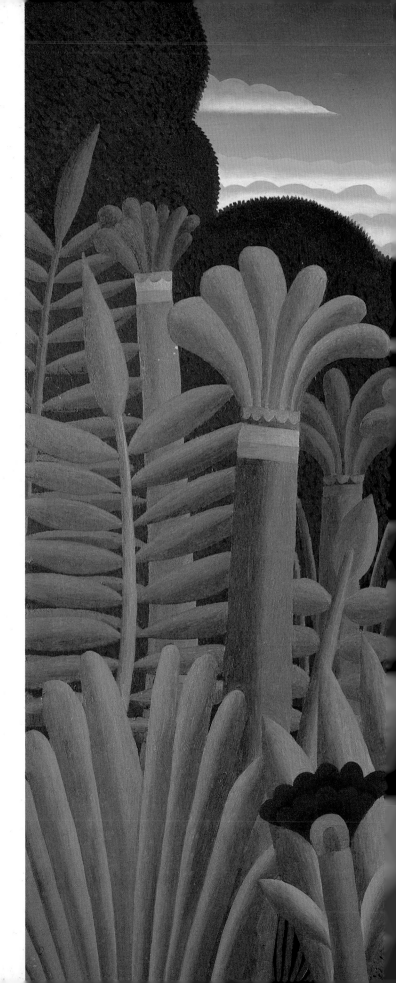

THE TIGER

Tiger! Tiger! burning bright
In the forests of the night,
What immortal hand or eye
Could frame thy fearful symmetry?

In what distant deeps or skies
Burnt the fire of thine eyes?
On what wings dare he aspire?
What the hand dare seize the fire?

And what shoulder, and what art,
Could twist the sinews of thy heart?
And when thy heart began to beat,
What dread hand? and what dread feet?

What the hammer? what the chain?
In what furnace was thy brain?
What the anvil? what dread grasp
Dare its deadly terrors clasp?

When the stars threw down their spears,
And water'd heaven with their tears,
Did he smile his work to see?
Did he who made the Lamb make thee?

Tiger! Tiger! burning bright
In the forests of the night,
What immortal hand or eye,
Dare frame thy fearful symmetry?

WILLIAM BLAKE

Upon the Snail

She goes but softly, but she goeth sure;
    She stumbles not as stronger creatures do:
Her journey's shorter, so she may endure
    Better than they which do much further go.

She makes no noise, but stilly seizeth on
    The flower or herb appointed for her food,
The which she quietly doth feed upon,
    While others range, and gare, but find no good.

And though she doth but very softly go,
    However 'tis not fast, nor slow, but sure;
And certainly they that do travel so,
    The prize they do aim at, they do procure.

JOHN BUNYAN

26

THE POOR MAN'S PIG

Already fallen plum-bloom stars the green,
   And apple-boughs as knarred as old toads' backs
Wear their small roses ere a rose is seen;
   The building thrush watches old Job who stacks
The bright-peeled osiers on the sunny fence,
   The pent sow grunts to hear him stumping by,
And tries to push the bolt and scamper thence,
   But her ringed snout still keeps her to the sty.

Then out he lets her run; away she snorts
   In bundling gallop for the cottage door,
With hungry hubbub begging crusts and orts,
   Then like the whirlwind bumping round once more;
Nuzzling the dog, making the pullets run,
And sulky as a child when her play's done.

EDMUND BLUNDEN

WORMS AND THE WIND

Worms would rather be worms.
Ask a worm and he says, "Who knows what a worm knows?"
Worms go down and up and over and under.
Worms like tunnels.
When worms talk they talk about the worm world.
Worms like it in the dark.
Neither the sun nor the moon interests a worm.
Zigzag worms hate circle worms.
Curve worms never trust square worms.
Worms know what worms want.
Slide worms are suspicious of crawl worms.
One worm asks another, "How does your belly drag today?"
The shape of a crooked worm satisfies a crooked worm.
A straight worm says, "Why not be straight?"
Worms tired of crawling begin to slither.
Long worms slither farther than short worms.
Middle-sized worms say, "It is nice to be neither long nor short."
Old worms teach young worms to say, "Don't be sorry for me unless you
    have been a worm and lived in worm places and read worm books."
When worms go to war they dig in, come out and
    fight, dig in again, come out and fight again, dig in again, and so on.
Worms underground never hear the wind overground
    and sometimes they ask, "What is this wind we hear of?"

CARL SANDBURG

28

THE RABBIT

The rabbit has a charming face:
Its private life is a disgrace.
I really dare not name to you
The awful things that rabbits do;
Things that your paper never prints –
You only mention them in hints.
They have such lost, degraded souls
No wonder they inhabit holes;
When such depravity is found
It only can live underground.

In part anon. and partly by
NAOMI ROYDE SMITH

ON A CAT AGEING

He blinks upon the hearth-rug
And yawns in deep content,
Accepting all the comforts
That Providence has sent.

Louder he purrs, and louder,
In one glad hymn of praise,
For all the night's adventures,
For quiet, restful days.

Life will go on for ever,
With all that cat can wish;
Warmth, and the glad procession
Of fish, and milk and fish.

Only – the thought disturbs him –
He's noticed once or twice,
The times are somehow breeding
A nimbler race of mice.

ALEXANDER GRAY

30

CAT AT THE CREAM

Jean, Jean, Jean,
The cat's at the cream,
Suppin wi her forefeet,
And glowrin wi her een!

ANON.

THE CAT'S SONG

Dirdum drum,
Three threads and a thrum,
Thrum gray, thrum gray.

ANON.

CAMELS OF THE KINGS

"The Camels, the Kings' Camels, Haie-aie!
Saddles of polished leather, stained red and purple,
Pommels inlaid with ivory and beaten gold,
Bridles of silk embroidery, worked with flowers.
The Camels, the Kings' Camels!"

We are groomed with silver combs,
We are washed with perfumes.
The grain of richest Africa is fed to us,
Our dishes are silver.
Like cloth-of-gold glisten our sleek pelts.
Of all camels, we alone carry the Kings!
Do you wonder that we are proud?
That our hooded eyes are contemptuous?

As we sail past the tented villages
They beat their copper gongs after us.
"The windswift, the desert racers. See them!
Faster than gazelles, faster than hounds,
Haie-aie! The Camels, the Kings' Camels!"
The sand drifts in puffs behind us,
The glinting quartz, the fine, hard grit.
Do you wonder that we look down our noses?
Do you wonder we flare our superior nostrils?

All night we have run under the moon,
Without effort, breathing lightly,
Smooth as a breeze over the desert floor,
One white star our compass.
We have come to no palace, no place
Of towers and minarets and the calling of servants,
But a poor stable in a poor town.
So why are we bending our crested necks?
Why are our proud heads bowed
And our eyes closed meekly?
Why are we outside this hovel,
Humbly and awkwardly kneeling?
How is it that we know the world is changed?

LESLIE NORRIS

HARES AT PLAY

The birds are gone to bed, the cows are still
And sheep lie panting on each old mole hill;
And underneath the willow's grey-green bough –
Like toil a-resting – lies the fallow plough;
The timid hares throw daylight's fears away
On the lane's road to dust and dance and play
Then dabble in the grain, by nought deterred,
To lick the dewfall from the barley's beard;
Then out they sturt again and round the hill,
Like happy thoughts dance squat and loiter still,
Till milking maidens in the early morn
Gingle their yokes and start them in the corn;
Through well known beaten paths each nimbling hare
Sturts quick as fear – and seeks its hidden lair.

JOHN CLARE

THE VIXEN

Among the taller wood with ivy hung,
The old fox plays and dances round her young;
She snuffs and barks if any passes by
And swings her tail and turns prepared to fly.
The horseman hurries by, she bolts to see,
And turns agen, from danger never free.
If any stands she runs among the poles
And barks and snaps and drives them in the holes;
The shepherd sees them and the boy goes by
And gets a stick and progs the hole to try;
They get all still and lie in safety sure,
And out again when everything's secure,
And start and snap at blackbirds bouncing by
To fight and catch the great white butterfly.

JOHN CLARE

FIRST SIGHT

Lambs that learn to walk in snow
When their bleating clouds the air
Meet a vast unwelcome, know
Nothing but a sunless glare.
Newly stumbling to and fro
All they find, outside the fold
Is a wretched width of cold.

As they wait beside the ewe,
Her fleeces wetly caked, there lies
Hidden round them, waiting too,
Earth's immeasurable surprise.
They could not grasp it if they knew,
What so soon will wake and grow
Utterly unlike the snow.

PHILIP LARKIN

THE JAGUAR

The apes yawn and adore their fleas in the sun.
The parrots shriek as if they were on fire, or strut
Like cheap tarts to attract the stroller with the nut.
Fatigued with indolence, tiger and lion

Lie still as the sun. The boa-constrictor's coil
Is a fossil. Cage after cage seems empty, or
Stinks of sleepers from the breathing straw.
It might be painted on a nursery wall.

But who runs like the rest past these arrives
At a cage where the crowd stands, stares, mesmerized,
As a child at a dream, at a jaguar hurrying enraged
Through prison darkness after the drills of his eyes

On a short fierce fuse. Not in boredom –
The eye satisfied to be blind in fire,
By the bang of blood in the brain deaf the ear –
He spins from the bars, but there's no cage to him

More than to the visionary his cell:
His stride is wildernesses of freedom:
The world rolls under the long thrust of his heel.
Over the cage floor the horizons come.

TED HUGHES

THE GAZELLE CALF

The gazelle calf, O my children,
goes behind its mother across the desert,
goes behind its mother on blithe bare foot
requiring no shoes, O my children!

D. H. LAWRENCE

THE PIED PIPER OF HAMELIN

1. The Cause.

Hamelin Town's in Brunswick,
By famous Hanover city;
The River Weser, deep and wide,
Washes its walls on the southern side;
A pleasanter spot you never spied;
But, when begins my ditty,
Almost five hundred years ago,
To see the townsfolk suffer so
From vermin, was a pity.

Rats!
They fought the dogs and killed the cats,
And bit the babies in the cradles,
And ate the cheeses out of the vats,
And licked the soup from the cooks' own ladles,
Split open the kegs of salted sprats,
Made nests inside men's Sunday hats,
And even spoiled the women's chats
By drowning their speaking
With shrieking and squeaking
In fifty different sharps and flats.

ROBERT BROWNING
from The Pied Piper of Hamelin

Two Performing Elephants

He stands with his forefeet on the drum
and the other, the old one, the pallid hoary female
must creep her great bulk beneath the bridge of him.

On her knees, in utmost caution
all agog, and curling up her trunk
she edges through without upsetting him.
Triumph! the ancient pig-tailed monster!

When her trick is to climb over him
with what shadow-like slow carefulness
she skims him, sensitive
as shadows from the ages gone and perished
in touching him, and planting her round feet.

While the wispy, modern children, half-afraid
watch silent. The looming of the hoary, far-gone ages
is too much for them.

D. H. LAWRENCE

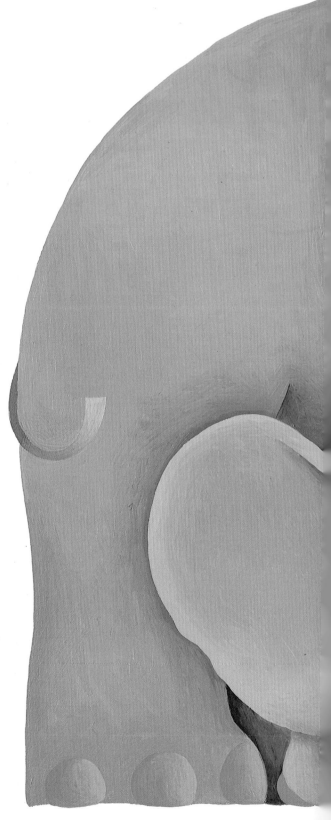

THE DUCK AND THE KANGAROO

Said the Duck to the Kangaroo,
  "Good gracious! how you hop!
Over the fields and the water too,
  As if you never would stop!
My life is a bore in this nasty pond,
And I long to go out in the world beyond!
  I wish I could hop like you!"
  Said the Duck to the Kangaroo.

"Please give me a ride on your back!"
  Said the Duck to the Kangaroo.
"I would sit quite still, and say nothing but 'Quack,'
  The whole of the long day through!
And we'd go to the Dee, and the Jelly Bo Lee,
Over the land, and over the sea; –
  Please take me a ride! O do!"
  Said the Duck to the Kangaroo.

Said the Kangaroo to the Duck,
  "This requires some little reflection;
Perhaps on the whole it might bring me luck,
  And there seems but one objection,
Which is, if you'll let me speak so bold,
Your feet are unpleasantly wet and cold,
And would probably give me the roo-
  Matiz!" said the Kangaroo.

Said the Duck, "As I sate on the rocks,
  I have thought over that completely,
And I bought four pairs of worsted socks
  Which fit my web-feet neatly.
And to keep out the cold I've bought a cloak,
And every day a cigar I'll smoke,
  All to follow my own dear true
  Love of a Kangaroo!"

Said the Kangaroo, "I'm ready!
  All in the moonlight pale;
But to balance me well, dear Duck, sit steady!
  And quite at the end of my tail!"
So away they went with a hop and a bound,
And they hopped the whole world three times round;
  And who so happy, – O who,
  As the Duck and the Kangaroo?

EDWARD LEAR

44

LIZARD

A lizard ran out on a rock and looked up, listening
no doubt to the sounding of the spheres.
And what a dandy fellow! the right toss of a chin for you
And swirl of a tail!

If men were as much men as lizards are lizards
they'd be worth looking at.

D. H. LAWRENCE

THE COW

The cow is of the bovine ilk;
One end is moo, the other, milk.

OGDEN NASH

Four stiff standers,
Four lily landers,
Two lookers, two crookers,
And a wig-wag.

ANON.

THE ASS IN THE LION'S SKIN

An Ass put on a Lion's skin and went
About the forest with much merriment,
Scaring the foolish beasts by brooks and rocks,
Till at last he tried to scare the Fox.
But Reynard, hearing from beneath the mane
That raucous voice so petulant and vain,
Remarked, "O Ass, I too would run away,
But that I know your old familiar bray."

That's just the way with asses, just the way.

AESOP
Rendered into verse by
WILLIAM ELLERY LEONARD

THE FLOWER-FED BUFFALOES

The flower-fed buffaloes of the spring
In the days of long ago,
Ranged where the locomotives sing
And the prairie flowers lie low:–
The tossing, blooming, perfumed grass
Is swept away by the wheat,
Wheels and wheels and wheels spin by
In the spring that still is sweet.
But the flower-fed buffaloes of the spring
Left us, long ago.
They gore no more, they bellow no more,
They trundle around the hills no more:–
With the Blackfeet, lying low,
With the Pawnees, lying low,
Lying low.

VACHEL LINDSAY

48

BUFFALO DUSK

The buffaloes are gone.
And those who saw the buffaloes are gone.
Those who saw the buffaloes by thousands and
    how they pawed the prairie sod into dust
    with their hoofs, their great heads down
    pawing on in a great pageant of dusk,
Those who saw the buffaloes are gone.
And the buffaloes are gone.

CARL SANDBURG

A Prayer To Go To Paradise With The Donkeys

to Maire and Jack

When I must come to you, O my God, I pray
It be some dusty-roaded holiday,
And even as in my travels here below,
I beg to choose by what road I shall go
To Paradise, where the clear stars shine by day.
I'll take my walking-stick and go my way,
And to my friends the donkeys I shall say,
"I am Francis Jammes, and I'm going to Paradise,
For there is no hell in the land of the loving God."
And I'll say to them: "Come, sweet friends of the blue skies,
Poor creatures who with a flap of the ears or a nod
Of the head shake off the buffets, the bees, the flies . . ."
Let me come with these donkeys, Lord, into your land,
These beasts who bow their heads so gently, and stand
With their small feet joined together in a fashion
Utterly gentle, asking your compassion.
I shall arrive, followed by their thousands of ears,
Followed by those with baskets at their flanks,
By those who lug the carts of mountebanks
Or loads of feather-dusters and kitchen-wares,
By those with humps of battered water-cans,
By bottle-shaped she-asses who halt and stumble,
By those tricked out in little pantaloons
To cover their wet, blue galls where flies assemble
In whirling swarms, making a drunken hum.
Dear God, let it be with these donkeys that I come,
And let it be that angels lead us in peace
To leafy streams where cherries tremble in air,
Sleek as the laughing flesh of girls; and there
In that haven of souls let it be that, leaning above
Your divine waters, I shall resemble these donkeys,
Whose humble and sweet poverty will appear
Clear in the clearness of your eternal love.

FRANCIS JAMMES
Translated from the French by
RICHARD WILBUR

PIKE

Pike, three inches long, perfect
Pike in all parts, green tigering the gold.
Killers from the egg: the malevolent aged grin.
They dance on the surface among the flies.

Or move, stunned by their own grandeur
Over a bed of emerald, silhouette
Of submarine delicacy and horror.
A hundred feet long in their world.

In ponds, under the heat-struck lily pads –
Gloom of their stillness:
Logged on last year's black leaves, watching upwards.
Or hung in an amber cavern of weeds

The jaws' hooked clamp and fangs
Not to be changed at this date;
A life subdued to its instrument;
The gills kneading quietly, and the pectorals.

Three we kept behind glass,
Jungled in weed: three inches, four,
And four and a half: fed fry to them –
Suddenly there were two. Finally one.

With a sag belly and the grin it was born with.
And indeed they spare nobody.
Two, six pounds each, over two feet long,
High and dry and dead in the willow-herb –

One jammed past its gills down the other's gullet:
The outside eye stared: as a vice locks –
The same iron in this eye
Though its film shrank in death.

A pond I fished, fifty yards across,
Whose lilies and muscular tench
Had outlasted every visible stone
Of the monastery that planted them –

Stilled legendary depth:
It was as deep as England. It held
Pike too immense to stir, so immense and old
That past nightfall I dared not cast

But silently cast and fished
With the hair frozen on my head
For what might move, for what eye might move.
The still splashes on the dark pond,

Owls hushing the floating woods
Frail on my ear against the dream
Darkness beneath night's darkness had freed,
That rose slowly towards me, watching.

TED HUGHES

THE WALRUS

The Walrus lives on icy floes
And unsuspecting Eskimoes.

Don't bring your wife to Arctic Tundra
A Walrus may bob up from undra.

MICHAEL FLANDERS

THE WATERBEETLE

The waterbeetle here shall teach
A sermon far beyond your reach:
He flabbergasts the Human Race
By gliding on the water's face
With ease, celerity, and grace;
But if he ever stopped to think
Of how he did it, he would sink.

HILAIRE BELLOC

THE OCTOPUS

Tell me, O Octopus, I begs,
Is those things arms, or is they legs?
I marvel at thee, Octopus;
If I were thou, I'd call me Us.

OGDEN NASH

FISH RIDDLE

Although it's cold no clothes I wear,
Frost and snow I do not fear,
I have no use for hose or shoes
Although I travel far and near.
All I eat comes free to me,
I need no cider, ale or sack,
I nothing buy or sell or lack.

ANON.
(A herring in the sea)

TIDINGS

In the Dogger's swirls
　Where the current whirls
　The hapless swarms of fry,
I dream of the sunlit harbours
　I knew in the months gone by.
For the sand eel and the squid peel
And the slivers of silver scales
　No longer drift
　As a guileless gift
That the tyro's hand impales.

On the Goodwin Shoal
Where the simple sole
　Has never put hook to mouth,
I wait for the summer season
　To come to the shores of the South.
For the rag worm and the lug worm
And the mussel dangling free
　But thinly fall
　From the harbour wall
And raggedly fringe the quay.

When the boats ply
And the flags fly
　I shall swim to the rod-ring'd piers,
Where fishermen flail
From the crowded rail
　(To tunes from "The Gondoliers"):
For the gay life is the short life
Nor sad is the inshore wave
　When all may dine
　From a baited line –
At the risk of a waterless grave.

MARK BEVAN

THE FISH

In a cool curving world he lies
And ripples with dark ecstasies.
The kind luxurious lapse and steal
Shapes all his universe to feel
And know and be; the clinging stream
Closes his memory, glooms his dream,
Who lips the roots o' the shore, and glides
Superb on unreturning tides.
Those silent waters weave for him
A fluctuant mutable world and dim,
Where wavering masses bulge and gape
Mysterious, and shape to shape
Dies momently through whorl and hollow,
And form and line and solid follow
Solid and line and form to dream
Fantastic down the eternal stream;
An obscure world, a shifting world,
Bulbous, or pulled to thin, or curled,
Or serpentine, or driving arrows,
Or serene slidings, or March narrows.
There slipping wave and shore are one,
And weed and mud. No ray of sun,
But glow to glow fades down the deep
(As dream to unknown dream in sleep);
Shaken translucency illumes
The hyaline of drifting glooms;
The strange soft-handed depth subdues
Drowned colour there, but black to hues,
As death to living, decomposes –
Red darkness of the heart of roses,
Blue brilliant from dead starless skies,
And gold that lies behind the eyes,
The unknown unnameable sightless white
That is the essential flame of night,
Lustreless purple, hooded green,
The myriad hues that lie between
Darkness and darkness! . . .

But there the night is close, and there
Darkness is cold and strange and bare;
And the secret deeps are whisperless;
And rhythm is all deliciousness;
And joy is in the throbbing tide,
Whose intricate fingers beat and glide
In felt bewildering harmonies
Of trembling touch; and music is
The exquisite knocking of the blood.
Space is no more, under the mud;
His bliss is older than the sun.
Silent and straight the waters run.
The lights, the cries, the willows dim,
And the dark tide are one with him.

RUPERT BROOKE
from The Fish

GLOSSARY

ACKNOWLEDGEMENTS

"A Prayer to go to Paradise with the Donkeys" by Francis Jammes, translated by Richard Wilbur, from *Poems 1934-56* by Richard Wilbur. Reprinted by permission of Faber and Faber Ltd.

"Buffalo Dusk" from *Smoke and Steel* by Carl Sandburg, © 1920 by Harcourt Brace Jovanovich, Inc. and renewed 1948 by Carl Sandburg, reprinted by permission of Harcourt Brace Jovanovich, Inc.

"Camels of the Kings" by Leslie Norris. Reprinted by permission of the author.

"Captive Bird" by Boethius, translated by Helen Waddell, from *More Latin Lyrics*, edited by Dame Felicitas Corrigan (Victor Gollancz Ltd, 1976), © Stanbrook Abbey 1976. Reprinted by permission of the editor.

"First Sight" by Philip Larkin, from *The Whitsun Weddings* by Philip Larkin, © 1964 Philip Larkin. Reprinted by permission of Faber and Faber Ltd.

"Flying Crooked" by Robert Graves from *Collected Poems* (1975), © 1975 Robert Graves. Reprinted by permission of A.P. Watt Ltd on behalf of the Executors of the Estate of Robert Graves.

"Night Heron" by Frances Frost from *The Little Naturalist*, Frost and Werth (1959, 1987). Reprinted by permission of the McGraw-Hill Publishing Company.

"Pike" by Ted Hughes, from *Lupercal,* © 1959, 1960 Ted Hughes. Reprinted by permission of Faber and Faber Ltd.

"The Ass in the Lion's Skin" by Aesop, rendered into verse by William Ellery Leonard, from *Aesop and Hyssop, Being Fables Adapted and Originated with the Morals carefully Formulated* (1912, 1963). Reprinted by permission of Open Court Publishing Company, La Salle, Illinois.

"The Bat" by Ruth Pitter, from *Collected Poems 1926-1966* by Ruth Pitter (Crescent Press, 1968). Reprinted by permission of Barrie and Jenkins Ltd.

"The Common Cormorant" by Christopher Isherwood, © 1966 Christopher Isherwood. Reproduced by permission of Curtis Brown, London, on behalf of the Estate of Christopher Isherwood.

"The Cow" by Odgen Nash, © Ogden Nash. Reproduced by permission of Curtis Brown, London, on behalf of the Estate of Ogden Nash.

"The Flower-Fed Buffaloes" by Vachel Lindsay, from *Going-to-the-Stars* by Vachel Lindsay, © 1926 by D. Appleton & Co., renewed 1954 by Elizabeth C. Lindsay. A Hawthorn Book. Reprinted by permission of Dutton, an imprint of New American Library, a division of Penguin Books USA Inc.

"The Jaguar" by Ted Hughes, from *The Hawk in the Rain,* © 1956, 1957 Ted Hughes. Reprinted by permission of Faber and Faber Ltd.

"The Manoeuvre" by William Carlos Williams from *Collected Poems volume 1 1939-1962,* © 1944, 1962 William Carlos Williams. Reprinted by permission of Carcanet Press Ltd.

"The Octopus" by Ogden Nash, © Ogden Nash. Reproduced by permission of Curtis Brown, London, on behalf of the Estate of Ogden Nash.

"The Poor Man's Pig" by Edmund Blunden, from *Selected Poems* edited by Robyn Marsack. Reprinted by permission of Carcanet Press Ltd.

"The Vulture" by Hilaire Belloc, from *More Beasts for Worse Children* (Gerald Duckworth & Co. Ltd, 1910, reprinted 1973). Reprinted by permission of the Peters Fraser and Dunlop Group Ltd.

"The Walrus" by Michael Flanders. Reprinted by permission of Claudia Flanders.

"The Waterbeetle" by Hilaire Belloc, from *A Moral Alphabet* (first published by Edward Arnold 1899; reissued by Gerald Duckworth & Co. Ltd, 1932). Reprinted by permission of the Peters Fraser and Dunlop Group Ltd.

"Tidings" by Mark Bevan, from *Punch* magazine, 6th December 1950. Reprinted by permission of Punch Publications Ltd.

"Worms and the Wind" by Carl Sandburg from *The Complete Poems of Carl Sandburg, Revised and Expanded Edition,* © 1950 by Carl Sandburg and renewed 1978 by Margaret Sandburg, Helga Sandburg Crile and Janet Sandburg, reprinted by permission of Harcourt Brace Jovanovich, Inc.

INDEX OF FIRST LINES

MORE WALKER PAPERBACKS
For You to Enjoy

Also illustrated by Reg Cartwright

PETER AND THE WOLF

retold by Selina Hastings

A lively retelling of Sergei Prokofiev's popular orchestral tale.

"Well told and richly illustrated." *The Good Book Guide*

0-7445-0990-4　£3.99

THE MAN WHO WANTED TO LIVE FOR EVER

retold by Selina Hastings

This colourful rendering of a classic European folk tale
is on the current recommended reading list of the
Standard Assessment Tests (SATs), Level 4.

"A good treatment of a good story." *The Daily Telegraph*

0-7445-2077-0　£4.99

THE CANTERBURY TALES

retold by Selina Hastings

A lively selection of seven of the best of Chaucer's tales.

"Reg Cartwright's characteristic combination of bold emblematic
figure drawing and lush Rousseauesque settings is just right...
Altogether, a glorious book." *Chris Powling, The Observer*

0-7445-3064-4　£6.99

**Walker Paperbacks are available from most booksellers, or by post from
Walker Books Ltd, PO Box 11, Falmouth, Cornwall TR10 9EN.**

To order, send: Title, author, ISBN number and price for each book ordered, your full name and address,
cheque or postal order for the total amount, plus postage and packing:

UK and BFPO Customers – £1.00 for first book, plus 50p for the second book and plus 30p for each additional book to a maximum charge of £3.00.
Overseas and Eire Customers – £2.00 for first book, plus £1.00 for the second book and plus 50p per copy for each additional book.
Prices are correct at time of going to press, but are subject to change without notice.